My HAPPY HEART

Prayer of the Heart

by Gregory Ryan

Afterword by Laurence Freeman, OSB

Medio
Media

Medio Media Publishing

Published by
Medio Medio Publishing
15930 N. Oracle Rd., Suite 196
Catalina, Arizona 85739

ISBN 0-9666941-9-8

Design and Illustrations by: Carlos Siqueira
Colors by: Sergio Peixoto Jr.
Visit our Website: http://sites.uol.com.br/csdg
E-mail: csdg@uol.com.br

In memory of Bridget Mara Horan

Whose happy heart

Now lives in all our hearts.

This book was made possible by the generous contributions

of the family of Eugenio Lopez Jr.

For the grandchildren of Eugenio Lopez Jr.

May they learn to love meditation as he did

My family loves me. I love my family.
My family works and plays together.
My family also prays together.

I help my mother and dad and the grownups who care for me.
I help my sisters and brothers.
My family loves me and I love my family.

In the morning and in the evening I sit in a quiet place. I sit still and close my eyes. I pray silently in my heart. Jesus...

I say the Holy Name of Jesus over and over in my heart.
Jesus... Jesus... Jesus... I do not hurry while I meditate.
Jesus... Jesus... Jesus...

God made my family and me.
Thank you, God, for giving me
a loving family.

My friends love me. I love my friends.
My friends and I play together.
We go to school together.
We help each other.

Sometimes my friends and I do not get along.
But my friends love me and I love my friends.

When I feel happy or when I feel sad,
I can sit still in my quiet place.
I close my eyes and pray the Holy Name of
Jesus in my heart. Jesus... Jesus... Jesus.

God made my friends and me.
Thank you, God, for giving me friends.

God loves me. I love God.
God has a plan for all people.
They should love one another.

Jesus was born for all people and
became our friend.
Jesus taught us that his Father
is our Father.
We are all children of God.

Jesus is our friend and brother.
He taught us to call God "Abba... Father..."

I meditate each day so I can
be with God in a special way.

I sit still in my quiet place. I close my eyes
and slowly pray the Holy Name of Jesus.

Jesus... Jesus... Jesus...

When I meditate, Jesus prays in my heart.
Jesus prays in my heart all through the day
and all through the night. He prays in my heart
even when I do not know it.

Whatever I do, Jesus prays in my heart. His prayer is Love.
Jesus and I pray together all the time.
Jesus... Jesus... Jesus...

I love myself. I take care of myself.

I eat healthy food and get a lot of exercise.

I study my best and play with my friends. I also rest and enjoy nature.

God made me. God made all things. All that God made is good.

Whenever I want to thank God I sit still in my quiet place and close my eyes and meditate.
I pray the Holy Name of Jesus. Jesus... Jesus... Jesus...

I love others. I have fun with other people. I learn many new things from other people. I enjoy animals, and nature and all the earth.

In my heart I love myself. I love my family and my friends.
In my heart I love God and people and all of creation.

I meditate every morning and every evening.
I can meditate with my family or I can meditate by myself.
In a quiet place I close my eyes and meditate.
Jesus... Jesus... Jesus...

When I meditate in silence... I am thanking God for making me.
I am thanking God for my family and my friends. I am thanking God
for my pets and other animals. I am thanking God for trees, flowers,
sun and clouds. I am thanking God for all of nature.
But when I meditate I do not think about any of this.
I simply pray
"Jesus... Jesus... Jesus..."

Every morning and evening
I sit still in my quiet place and close my eyes.
My heart is happy as I pray the Holy Name of Jesus.
Jesus... Jesus... Jesus...

For Parents and Teachers
The Tradition of Christian Meditation

The practice of Christian meditation has been handed down through the ages. The early desert monks and nuns would silently turn a single sacred word or phrase over and over in their heart. Through that simple act of love they entered into the very life of the Holy Trinity. In our own time this practice was rediscovered and revitalized for contemporary men, women and children by the late Benedictine monk, John Main (1926-1982). Father John, as he is known, had learned to meditate as a young man while serving in Malaya in the British Foreign Service. Like a humble child, he learned to meditate using the Sacred Name of Jesus. While it was a very simple practice, it was a practice that changed his life forever.

Years later, as a monk, John Main found the practice of meditation in his own Christian tradition. John Cassian, the author of *The Cloud of Unknowing* and other writers recommended the use of a sacred word or mantra, as it is called today, to bring the meditator into silence and stillness. *"Be still and know that I am God" (Psam 46).*

John Main traveled from his monastery in London to found a contemplative monastery that became the seed-bed for what is now known as *The World Community for Christian Meditation*, a kind of monastery without walls. Since John Main's death in 1982, Father Laurence Freeman OSB who co-founded the community with him has continued to direct the thousands of meditators, weekly meditation groups, and meditation centers around the world who have made the discipline of meditation a regular part of each day, in all walks of life.

How to Meditate

Sit down. Sit still and upright. Close your eyes lightly. Sit relaxed but alert. Silently, interiorly begin to say a single word. For adults we recommend the prayer phrase "maranatha". Recite it in faith as four syllables of equal length. "Ma-ra-na-tha". Listen to it as you say it, gently but continuously.

The mantra is an Aramaic word - which is the language Jesus spoke - found at the end of the First Letter to the Corinthians and at the end of the Book of Revelation. It means, "Come, Lord!" But during the time of meditation, do not think or imagine anything - spiritual or otherwise. If thoughts and images come, these are distractions at the time of meditation, so keep returning to simply saying the word. Meditate each morning and evening for between twenty and thirty minutes.

Children and Meditation

How long should your child meditate? John Main recommended a minute of meditation for each year of the child's age. A seven year old would meditate for seven minutes each morning and evening. A twelve year old would meditate for twelve minutes, and so on. The optimum time for adults is thirty minutes.

It would be best to meditate together as a family each day, depending on your schedules. You might begin with a short spontaneous prayer or a reading from scripture. After the appropriate time has elapsed, you would gently touch the child's knee signaling the end of their meditation. He or she could then go to their room to play quietly, paint, or read while you and the older children continued to meditate. The twice-daily periods of meditation will become a normal part of each day - just like meals, playtime, and homework.

John Main felt that all children possess an innate genius which should be carefully guarded and nurtured by grownups. All too soon it may be trampled on by society. He was also convinced of a need for a daily discipline of prayer like Christian meditation in each child's life. However just as a flower opens in its own good time, children must be free to come to meditation in their own good time. All of them need the freedom to find their own level of commitment day-to-day. Do not force them.

On Saturday mornings Father John met with a group of children at the monastery. He would often play imaginative games with them. Once for example he told them that the comb which he took out of his back pocket was magic. "If you draw it through your hair, your hair will turn into gold." One boy exclaimed, "Say, give me that. I've always wanted gold hair."

The small group then meditated together. There was no question about the naturalness of meditating. They sat simply and quietly in faith. Meditation seemed as natural to the children as breathing. And as simple.

There is a great lesson here. What is required of each of us - whether seven, seventeen, or seventy - is to recapture that natural, childlike simplicity and faith.

"Unless you become like a little child, you cannot enter the Kingdom."

The World Community for Christian Meditation

Meditation creates community. Since John Main started the first Christian Mediation Centre in 1975, a steadily growing community of Christian meditators has spread around the world.

The International Centre in London co-ordinates the worldwide community of meditators. A quarterly newsletter giving spiritual teaching and reflection is sent out from London and distributed from a number of national centers, together with local and international news of retreats and other events being held in the world-wide community. An annual John Main Seminar is held. The International Centre is funded entirely by donations and especially through a Friends of the International Centre programme

There are thousands of meditators around the world, as well as hundreds of weekly meditation groups and over a dozen Meditation Centers. You may obtain a quarterly newsletter and a catalogue of books, audiotapes and videotapes on Christian meditation by John Main OSB, Laurence Freeman OSB and others by contacting:

UNITED KINGDOM
The World Community for Christian Meditation International Centre
23 Kensington Square
London W8 5HN / United Kingdom
Tel +44 207 937 4679   Fax.+44 20/ 937 6790
E-mail: **wccm@compuserve.com**

UNITED STATES NATIONAL CENTER
15930 N. Oracle Road Ste 196
Tucson AZ 85/39 USA
Toll Free in US 1-888-673-7770
E-mail   WCCM@mediomedia.com

Catalog:
Medio Media Publishing
15930 N. Oracle Ste 196
Catalina, AZ 85739
1-877-285-6809
E-mail: **meditation@mediomedia.com**

WEB PAGE
Visit *The World Community for Christian Meditation Web site* for information, weekly meditation group readings and discussion at

Visit *Medio Media Web site* to order books, audio, video tapes, and music for meditation at

Medio Media is the publishing arm of The World Community for Christian Meditation. It is committed to the dissemination of the teaching of meditation in the Christian tradition and, in particular to the work of John Main. It is further committed to the growing dialogue among meditators and seekers from all traditions based on the experience of silence shared by all religions.

The World
Community for
Christian
Meditation

Afterword by Laurence Freeman, OSB

The very young - and sometimes the very old - are the best students of meditation

One of my best teachers of meditation was a small group of children who I was once asked to introduce to this way of pure and simple prayer. At first I was very reluctant to do so. Meditation seemed to be a very mature way of prayer. Then, even after starting the group and being surprised at how naturally the children seemed to take to it, I was a bit bemused by their response after the meditation period. Or rather lack of response as they had no questions – or comments. So I wondered if they were really doing it at all. Maybe they were just being polite. But when I asked them to introduce newcomers to the group to meditation I was astonished at how clearly they had grasped it. They taught me in a way I could not question that meditation is simple and natural and that if we do not become like little children we will never get into the kingdom of heaven. Since then I have welcomed the opportunity to teach meditation to the very young and to adolescents because I have seen how much they thirst for this teaching and experience their own spirit and how eagerly they respond. It is a wonder and joy to see many children's meditation groups spring up around our worldwide community.

As a schoolteacher, Greg Ryan has a professional interest in children and knowledge about them. But he is also a teacher of meditation and disciple of John Main. Bringing these aspects to his life together has resulted in this beautiful and valuable book that can open the treasures of our tradition of prayer to the young, the very people we must be concerned about for the future of our world. There is nothing more important to teach them than how to find and enter and stay in tune with their own heart. To live with a spiritual vision. To sense the sacredness of life, to see God in and behind everyday appearences. In the process of teaching what should always be taught as a priority to the young we, the parents and teachers, may learn a lot about what we should never have forgotten.

Laurence

Laurence Freeman, OSB
Director of The World
Community for Christian Meditation